BELLEVILLE And NUTLEY IN THE CIVIL WAR

a Brief History

CAPT. HENRY BENSON, U.S.A.
BORN NOV. 20TH 1824
DIED AUG. 11TH 1862

FRANCES E. BENSON
BORN JULY 29TH 1826
DIED SEPT. 15TH 1873

ANNIE DIED DEC. 10TH 1868
IN THE 23RD YEAR OF HER AGE

By Anthony Buccino

Belleville and Nutley in the Civil War, a Brief History

Copyright © 2011-2017 by Anthony Buccino

Second Edition V 3.2017

Cherry Blossom Press, PO Box 110252, Nutley NJ 07110

ISBN-10 0982567790   ISBN-13 978-0982567791

KINDLE ISBN 10 0982567774 ISBN-13 9780982567777

A small booklet about the towns' participation in the War Between the States, adapted from *BELLEVILLE SONS HONOR ROLL Remembering the Men Who Paid For Our Freedom, NUTLEY SONS HONOR ROLL Remembering the Men Who Paid For Our Freedom* and other sources. Franklin, now known as Nutley, was a part of Belleville until 1874.

DISCLAIMER: While every effort has been made to check and crosscheck references and sources, conflicts and omissions may occur. We welcome additions, corrections and supplemental information for inclusion in future editions. Provided links are subject to change.

Nonfiction, Civil War, War Between the States, Second River, Belleville, Nutley, New Jersey, Military history, Civil War diary, Essex County.

Front and interior photos by Anthony Buccino: Capt. Henry Benson headstone, Reformed Dutch Church of Second River cemetery, Belleville, N.J., Civil War memorial, Franklin Avenue, Nutley.

Special thanks to Michael Perrone, Belleville Historical Society

Visit BellevilleSons.com or Nutleysons.com

Belleville and Nutley in the Civil War a Brief History

Foreword 6

In The Beginning 8

Belleville Men Killed In Action 9

Veterans Of Belleville 16

Diary of James C. Taylor 20

39th Regiment - Infantry - Volunteers 34

Nutley (Franklin) Men Killed In Action 36

On Far-Flung Battlefields Nutley's Sons Died 42

Call For Volunteers 45

Veterans of Nutley 47

Acknowledgements 49

About the Editor 54

Belleville and Nutley in the Civil War, a Brief History

A small booklet about Belleville and Nutley (Franklin), New Jersey's participation in the War of the Rebellion, 1861-1865, adapted from

BELLEVILLE SONS HONOR ROLL

Remembering the Men Who Paid For Our Freedom,

NUTLEY SONS HONOR ROLL

Remembering the Men Who Paid For Our Freedom

and other sources.

Belleville Men
Killed In Action

Thomas Stevens (Stephens) was killed June 27, 1862

Captain Henry Benson died August 11, 1862

John Rogers (Rodgers) died April 8, 1865

Nutley (Franklin) Men
Killed In Action

Sgt. John Donaldson, May 17, 1862

Byron Lawton, September 14, 1862

James H. Cunningham, May 3, 1863

Oh! thus be it ever, when freemen shall stand

Between their loved home and the war's desolation!

Blest with victory and peace, may the heav'n rescued land

Praise the Power that hath made

and preserved us a nation.

Then conquer we must, when our cause it is just,

And this be our motto: "In God is our trust."

And the star-spangled banner in triumph shall wave

O'er the land of the free and the home of the brave!

Star Spangled Banner – Francis Scott Key, 1814

Dedicated to the Belleville

and Nutley (Franklin) sons

and daughters

who paid for our freedom,

and those who made the supreme sacrifice,

and the high cause they served.

We thank all our veterans.

Foreword

Records indicate 1.5 million Americans died in the War of Secession – nearly 700,000 in battle or from disease – which raged from 1861 to 1865. Newark, N.J., sent 10,000 men into the Union Army. New Jersey provided 88,000 troops and $26 million for the war. More than 6,000 New Jersey men died in the war.

The full number of men from Belleville and Nutley (still a part of Belleville), N.J., who served during the war is difficult to determine. Many local men joined the service in New York and other locations as they saw the New Jersey militia as too slow in activating its troops. Here, we try to include many of the names and units of local men who fought 150 years ago for the preservation of the Union.

We do know that six men, three each from Belleville and Nutley (Franklin), perished on the battlefield.

From Belleville, two soldiers died in the Seven Days' Battle (Peninsula Campaign) as Thomas Stevens (Stephens) was killed June 27, 1862, and Captain Henry Benson died of his wounds on August 11, 1862.

John Rogers (Rodgers) was killed in action on April 8, 1865, at Fort Davis while defending Washington, D.C., shortly before the war ended.

From Nutley (Franklin), then part of Belleville, Sgt. John Donaldson died May 17, 1862, in the first pitched battle of the Peninsula Campaign, known as the Battle of Williamsburg, Va., and the battle of Fort Magruder.

Byron Lawton died September 14, 1862, in the Battle of South Mountain, or the Battle of Burkittsville in Central Maryland during the Maryland Campaign.

James H. Cunningham died May 3, 1863, in the Second Battle of Fredericksburg, also known as the Second Battle of Marye's Heights.

In northeast New Jersey, Newark was founded in 1666, and included the area that would later become present-day Belleville and Nutley.

According to Frank Speer in *Nutley Was Born in Strife, Strategy and Secession*, in 1812, the northern half of Newark seceded and became part of Bloomfield, until 1839 when the eastern third broke off to form Belleville which was centered on the Second River.

Nutley came to be known as North Belleville. Due to taxation without representation, the people of what is now Nutley hated Belleville so much that they refused the name North Belleville and took the name of Franklinville in honor of Benjamin Franklin's only son, William, New Jersey's last royal governor. A separate town was chartered in 1874, when Franklinville became Franklin. As early as 1849, Franklinville had its own Post Office.

Many veterans of the Civil War are buried in Nutley at the Franklin Reformed Church Cemetery on Church Street and the (Saint Vincent Cemetery), Vincent United Methodist Church Cemetery on Passaic Avenue, where services are held each year on Memorial Day.

Founded by Dutch settlers in 1697, the Belleville Reformed Church was originally known as the Old Dutch Church of Second River and is located on Rutgers Street, or Belleville Turnpike, near the Passaic River. The church tower was used to spy on British troops across the river during the American Revolution. In its cemetery are buried 66 veterans of that war. Civil War casualty Captain Henry Benson is interred here. A memorial is held at the cemetery on the Fourth of July.

Other Civil War veterans are buried at Christ Church Episcopal Cemetery on Main Street in Belleville.

As with all collections of this type, new items of information are forever being uncovered and added to fill out our knowledge of our history. More detailed information about regiments and battles can also be found online. For now, let us use this booklet to remember and discuss the participation of Belleville and Nutley in the preservation of the United States.

Sources: *Civil War Diary of James C. Taylor of Belleville, Company F, 39th Regiment, New Jersey Volunteers, in the War to Save the Union of the United States of America, 1925.*

Wikipedia: http://en.wikipedia.org/wiki/Battle_of_Williamsburg

- http://en.wikipedia.org/wiki/Second_Battle_of_Fredericksburg

- http://en.wikipedia.org/wiki/Battle_of_Crampton%27s_Gap

National Park Service http://www.nps.gov/cwdw/historyculture/fort-davis.htm

In The Beginning

The call for volunteers in 1862 found Franklin a part of Belleville. A small military company of about forty men had been drilling for some time under Cornelius McClees, in the old school house on Avondale Road.

Twenty-six of this little company immediately volunteered and with fourteen others from Belleville marched with McClees to Camp Frelinghuysen in Newark. The camp served as rendezvous and drill ground for volunteer regiments of the state. According to a commemorative plaque at the site, it lay within the tract bounded by the Morris Canal, Orange Street, Roseville and Bloomfield avenues.

Here they were mustered into the State Service on September 3, 1862, and were enrolled in Company C of the 26th New Jersey Volunteers for nine months.

The regiment was made up of men from adjoining towns, Orange, South Orange, Bloomfield and Caldwell, each furnishing one company, while Newark furnished the remaining six. Three weeks later, after they were officered and equipped, they proceeded to Washington.

Samuel H. Pemberton, of Newark, was chosen captain of Company C and Cornelius McClees First Lieutenant.

The "26th of New Jersey" was in three engagements before Fredericksburg, Va., the great defeat of the Union troops, under General Burnside, on December 13, 1862, and the two minor engagements of May 3 and June 5, 1863, under General Hooker.

In the great battle of Dec. 13th, as raw troops, they faced the terrific fire of the Confederate batteries, and for three nights lay down upon their arms. They also took part in the memorable "mud march" back to camp. After the season in winter quarters near Belle Plain, Va., they again took the field, and eventually captured and held the Heights of Fredericksburg.

The regiment returned to Newark when their term of enlistment expired and was mustered out Sept. 19, 1863.

Source: The History of Nutley, compiled by Elizabeth Stow Brown, The Woman's Public School Auxiliary; copyright 1907 by The Board of Education of Nutley, New Jersey. Full text of article appears later in this book. Camp Frelinghuysen description added.

Belleville Men Killed In Action

Civil War

Henry Benson

Captain Henry Benson, of Belleville, died August 11 of wounds received on July 1, 1862, at the battle of Malvern Hill, Va., the sixth and last of the Seven Days Battles (Peninsula Campaign). On that day, Confederate Gen. Robert E. Lee launched a series of disjointed assaults on the nearly impregnable Union position on Malvern Hill.

Malvern Hill was one of the North's rare victories in the early years of the Civil War. The Battle of Malvern Hill, also known as the Battle of Poindexter's Farm, took place on July 1, 1862, in Henrico County, Va. Fought during the Peninsula Campaign, it proved the superiority of Union artillery, which together with Union troops under the able leadership of Gen. Philip Kearny, decisively repulsed Robert E. Lee's attempt to destroy the Army of the Potomac.

Photograph from the main eastern theater of war, the Peninsular Campaign, May-August 1862. Standing, left to right: Lt. Edmund Pendleton, PLt. Alex C. M. Pennington, Capt. Henry Benson, Capt, H. M. Gibson, Lt. James E. Wilson, Capt. John C. Tidball, Lt. William N. Dennison. Seated, left to right: Capt. Horatio Gibson, Lt. Peter C. Hains, Lt. Col. William Hays, Capt. James M. Robertson, Lt. J. W. Barlow. Seated on the ground, left to right: Lt. Robert H. Chapin, Lt. Robert Clarke, A.C. Vincent.

Library of Congress photo

LOCAL INTELLIGENCE

CAPT. BENSON, U.S.A. – Among the sufferers placed on board the steamer Spaulding at Harrison's Landing, to be brought to Philadelphia, was Capt. Henry Benson, of the Second Regiment U.S. Artillery. He had a shell wound in the right thigh, received from one of his own guns at Malvern Hill on the 6th inst., from which, unfortunately, he died on board the boat. Captain Benson was from Belleville, in this State, and rose from the ranks. For his good qualities as a soldier he received a commission as a brevet second lieutenant of the Second Artillery, June 28th, 1848. In March, 1853, he was commissioned first lieutenant, and in May, 1861, captain. He was a fine artillery officer, and a favorite with Gen. McClellan and all with whom he was associated. The funeral will take place with military honors, to-morrow, at 3 P.M., from the Reformed Dutch Church in Belleville.

MILITARY FUNERAL AT BELLEVILE – A large concourse of people assembled yesterday at Belleville to pay their last respects to the memory of the late Capt. Benson, of the U.S. Army. The Pall Bearers were Maj. Gen. Runyon, Col. A.J. Johnson, Col. A.F. Munn, Col E.A. Carman, Lieut. Col. Swords, Lieut. Col. Corby of Bloomfield, Paymaster Ward, of Belleville, and Major Webster of Belleville. A detachment of 100 men from the 13th Regiment, a Company from Bloomfield, and one from Franklin formed the military escort. The remains were taken from the house to the Dutch Reformed Church, where the funeral ceremonies took place. After the services the body was carried to the grave yard in rear of the church, upon the shoulders of six men from the 13th Regiment, detailed for that purpose, and with measured step, and notes from the fife and drum, with the ceremonies of the Episcopal church, all that remains of the patriot was consigned to the grave – "dust to dust, ashes to ashes," there to remain until the resurrection. At the close of the services a volley of three rounds was fired over the grave by a platoon of men, and the vast assemblage retired, showing that the words of the text was verified "than thou destroyest the hope of man." *(Newark Daily Mercury, Aug.13.1862)*

The grave of Capt. Henry Benson, (November 20, 1824 to August 11, 1862), in the Dutch Reformed Church Cemetery, Belleville, N.J., is a few feet north of the marble obelisk marking the Benson family plot, located near the middle of the churchyard's western wall. His name appears on both the northern facade of the obelisk and on a separate marble headstone with Civil War imagery in its tympanum: a cannon, forager cap, and Old Glory.

The 38-year-old Civil War officer was a Belleville native, born in the Miller House, and was accorded his hometown's first military funeral. He was captain and commander of Battery M, 2nd United States Regular Light Artillery.

The battery between Forts Ripley and Mansfield, and west of Powder Mill Branch (Maryland) are to be called Battery Benson after Capt. Henry Benson, who died Aug. 11, 1982, of wounds received at the second engagement at Malvern Hill, Va., by order of Brig. Gen. George W. Cullum, Chief of Staff, March 16, 1863.

Another battery was named for Maj. Gen Philip Kearny, U.S. Volunteers, killed at the battle of Chantilly, Va.

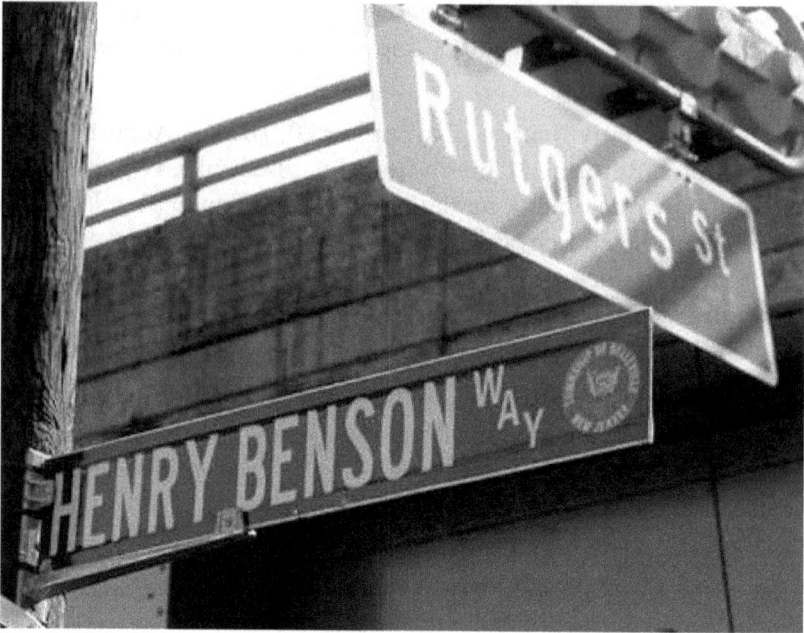

Henry Benson Way at the intersection of Main and Rutgers streets was dedicated in honor of Capt. Benson. The ceremony was held Sept. 10, 2016.

Sources: American Civil War.com; Belleville: 150th-Anniversary Historical Highlights 1839-1989 by Robert B. Burnett and the Belleville 150th-Anniversary Committee Belleville, New Jersey. 1991. Belleville Historical Society – Michael Perrone; Newark Daily Mercury, Weds., August 13, 1862, Local Intelligence and Military Funeral at Belleville, courtesy of Glen Pierce. Wikipedia: http://en.wikipedia.org/wiki/Battle_of_Malvern_Hill; http://en.wikipedia.org/wiki/File:Benson%27s_Battery_M_at_Fair_Oaks_1862 _-_LC-B815-433.JPG Find a Grave memorial; Created by: Nikita Barlow; Record added: Aug 01, 2002; Find A Grave Memorial# 6653672; http://www.findagrave.com/cgi-bin/fg.cgi?page=gr&GScid=1259891&GRid=6653672&

John J. Rogers (Rodgers)

John Rogers (Rodgers) was killed in action on April 8, 1865, at Fort Davis while defending Washington, D.C., shortly before the war ended.

Rogers, of Belleville, died of his wounds, according to the Civil War Diary of James C. Taylor of Belleville, Company F, 39th Regiment, New Jersey Volunteers, in the War to Save the Union of the United States of America.

In his diary, Taylor wrote on April 1: "At 11 last night 2 pieces of heavy artillery were brought into Fort Davis. This looks ominous. At 11:30 the regiment fell in and went out alongside the road where they waited there for hot coffee, and then we removed down to the front. We moved as far front as we could and then were ordered to lie flat on the ground. The enemy are firing lively with mortar shells and rifle shots. While lying flat, John Rodgers received a fatal wound."

Taylor enlisted in Captain John Hunkele's Company on Sept. 17, 1864, along with Rodgers, James M. Crisp, Linus Ackerman, Edmund Holmes, Charles Stanford, James McCluskey and Daniel McGinnis.

Before the war, the Union capital was a sleepy city of approximately 62,000 residents. The city sat almost completely unprotected, with Fort Washington, the lone fortification, being 12 miles south. Virginia, a Confederate state, lay on one side of the city, and Maryland, a slave-owning state, was on the other, leaving Washington dangerously vulnerable.

By 1865, the Defenses of Washington included 68 forts, supported by 93 detached batteries for field guns, 20 miles of rifle pits, and covered ways, wooden blockhouses at three key points, 32 miles of military roads, several stockaded bridgeheads, and four picket stations. Along the circumference of the 37-mile circle of fortifications were emplacements for a total of 1501 field and siege guns of which 807 guns and 98 mortars were in place. The defenseless city of 1860 had become one of the most heavily fortified cities of the world.

Private John J. Rogers enlisted Sept. 13, 1864, mustered in Sept. 25, 1864 for 1 year. He died at 3d Div. U. S. Army Gen. Hospital, Alexandria, Va., April 8, 1865, of wounds received in action before Petersburg, Va. He is buried at Alexandria National Cemetery, Alexandria, Alexandria City, Virginia, USA, and Plot: Company G, Thirty-ninth Regiment.

Sources: Civil War Diary of James C. Taylor of Belleville, Company F, 39th Regiment, New Jersey Volunteers, in the War to Save the Union of the United States

of America, 1925. National Park Service
http://www.nps.gov/cwdw/historyculture/fort-davis.htm Find A Grave Memorial#
10453303; Record added: Feb 10, 2005; http://www.findagrave.com/cgi-
bin/fg.cgi?page=gr&GSln=Rogers&GSfn=John&GSmn=J.&GSbyrel=all&GS
dy=1865&GSdyrel=in&GScntry=4&GSob=c&GRid=10453303&df=all&

Thomas Stevens (Stephens)

Color Sergeant Thomas J. Stevens (Stephens), of Belleville, was killed June 27, 1862, in The Battle of Gaines's Mill, sometimes known as the First Battle of Cold Harbor or the Battle of Chickahominy River, took place on June 27, 1862, in Hanover County, Virginia, as the third of the Seven Days Battles (Peninsula Campaign).

A member of the First New Jersey Brigade, he served under 1st Lt. W. E. Blewett in the Second Regiment. A color sergeant is a sergeant who carries the regimental, battalion, or national colors as in a color guard.

"Friday, June 27th, 1862, the First New Jersey Brigade was ordered to Woodbury's Bridge over the Chickohominy, there to meet Gen. Porter's Division. ... Col. Tucker led out the remaining four companies, including Lt. Blewett's command with the rest of the Brigade. From Woodbury's Bridge this Brigade, with others, was sent to engage the enemy near Gaines's Mills and was soon in the thick of the fight. Porter's Division, in hand-to-hand conflict, held their position against overwhelming odds until reinforcements, long delayed, arrived, but owing to the fact that their position was unfavorable and to the superiority of the enemy in numbers, the Union troops were compelled to retire. ... The Second Regiment had the right of line, and though outnumbered and flanked by the enemy, they were the last to leave their station in the field. In this fight the regiment lost its colonel, Isaac M. Tucker, Capt. Charles Danforth, Color Sergeant Thomas Stevens of Belleville, and many others. ..."

Sources C.C. Hine And His Times, Woodside, Pages 244 and 245 (Belleville Public Library); FIRST NEW JERSEY BRIGADE, Page 443 (aka Stephens); Wikipedia http://en.wikipedia.org/wiki/Battle_of_Gaines%27s_Mill

Veterans of Belleville

William E. Blewett

Born in New York City, William E. Blewett (1836 to 1913) came to Belleville at an early age. In the spring of 1861, just after the Civil War broke out, he organized a company of volunteer troops for service in the Union Army. The 101-man company, comprised mostly of Belleville men, arrived in Washington, D.C., in May.

Blewett's company, part of the First New Jersey Brigade, helped to cover the retreat of the Union Army after the first battle of Bull Run in Virginia two months later.

A second lieutenant in 1861, Blewett was made a first lieutenant by order of General Philip Kearny (for whom the town across the Passaic River is named) in 1862.

At the Battle of Gaines' Mill in June 1862, the Union troops sustained losses of nearly 6,000 killed and wounded at the hands of the Confederate Army; one of the dead was Color Sergeant Thomas Stevens of Belleville.

Blewett was shot in the chest but the bullet traveled down and lodged in his side. While returning to the rear for medical treatment, an exploding shell blew off his belt.

Blewett came home to Belleville on the Fourth of July. The fact that the bullet could not be located and removed prevented him from returning to active service.

He was commissioned as 2nd lieutenant of Company F, 2nd New Jersey Volunteer Infantry on June 12, 1861. He was promoted to 1st lieutenant on June 4, 1862 to replace Henry Vreeland, who had been advanced to captain. He resigned his commission on September 9, 1862.

Blewett served in the New Jersey National Guard and rose through the ranks to become a captain, major, and lieutenant colonel before resigning in 1874. A jeweler by trade, William E. Blewett died in 1913. He is buried at Mount Pleasant Cemetery, Newark, N.J.

Sources: American Civil War.com; Belleville: 150th-Anniversary Historical Highlights 1839-1989 by Robert B. Burnett and the Belleville 150th-Anniversary Committee Belleville, New Jersey, 1991. Find A Grave; Created by: Russ Dodge; Record added: Mar 12, 2004; Find Grave Memorial # 8497904.

http://www.findagrave.com/cgi-
bin/fg.cgi?page=gr&GSln=Blewett&GSfn=William+&GSmn=E&GSbyrel=al
l&GSdy=1913&GSdyrel=in&GScntry=4&GSob=c&GRid=8497904&df=
all&

Sgt. John Campbell

The grave of Civil War veteran John Campbell is marked by a GAR
medallion and a regulation military stone indicating that he had served in
the Army of the Potomac as a sergeant, Company F, 2nd New Jersey
Infantry. He is buried at Christ Church Cemetery, Belleville, N.J. Plot:
SE quarter of burial ground

*Source: Find A Grave, created by Nikita Barlow; Record added: March 27, 2004;
Find A Grave Memorial# 8564774; Find a Grave – Christ Church at
http://www.findagrave.com/cgi-
bin/fg.cgi?page=gr&GScid=1259911&GRid=8564774&*

Maj. Gen. Daniel Henry Rucker

Daniel Henry Rucker was born on April 28, 1812, at Belleville, New
Jersey. As a young man, he moved to Grosse Ile, Michigan, a village near
Detroit, and it was from Michigan that he was commissioned directly
into the U.S. Army as a 2nd Lieutenant of Dragoons on October 13,
1837.

For gallantry at Buena Vista in the Mexican War, he was promoted Major
and in 1849, he transferred from line duty to the staff of the
Quartermaster Department.

During the Civil War, he was promoted Brigadier General of Volunteers
in charge of the depot for the Quartermaster Department and oversaw
the procurement of the equipment needed for the transportation of an
Army for the course of the entire war.

For diligent and faithful service, he was brevetted Major General of US
Volunteers. After the war, he was appointed Assistant Quartermaster
General of the Army and in 1882, he was appointed Quartermaster
General of the Army. He retired that same year, after forty-five years of
duty.

Daniel Henry Rucker died on January 6 1910, in Washington, DC. He is buried at Arlington National Cemetery, Arlington, Virginia. Plot: Section 1, Grave 074.

Sources: US Civil War Generals at http://sunsite.utk.edu/civil-war/ung_r.html; http://www.arlingtoncemetery.net/dhrucker.html; Find A Grave; Record added: Oct 24, 2001; Find A Grave Memorial# 5885498; http://www.findagrave.com/cgi-bin/fg.cgi?page=gr&GSln=Rucker&GSfn=Daniel&GSmn=Henry&GSbyrel=all&GSdyrel=in&GScntry=4&GSob=c&GRid=5885498&df=all&; bio by: John "J-Cat" Griffith.

William Danforth Whiting

The Civil War Union naval officer was born in Lancaster, Mass., and is buried at Christ Church Cemetery, Main Street, Belleville, N.J.

According to a biography by Shirley Stanton, William Danforth Whiting (May 26, 1823 to March 19, 1894) entered the U.S. Navy on March 1, 1841 as a midshipman.

He attended the U.S. Naval Academy from 1847 to 1848 and was graduated. In 1855, he was promoted to lieutenant, and was serving on the steam frigate "Niagara" when the first Atlantic cable was laid in 1857.

After the outbreak of the Civil War, he served as the executive officer of the sloop "USS Vandalia" at the capture of Port Royal in 1861, and commanded the steamer "USS Wyandotte" on the South Atlantic blockade and in the Potomac flotilla.

Promoted to Lieutenant Commander in July 1862, he participated in the attacks on the defenses of Charleston while aboard the gunboat "USS Ottawa". From 1864 to 1865 he commanded the "USS Savannah" in the Eastern Gulf station.

He held a succession of commands after the war. On July 25, 1866, he received his commission as Commander and was aboard the steamer "USS Tioga", off the coast of Maine and in the Gulf.

He was based at the New York Navy Yard, in Brooklyn, New York from 1867 to 1869 and from 1871 to 1872. In the North Atlantic, between 1869 and 1870, he commanded the sloop "USS Saratoga" and the monitor "USS Miantonomoh" (one of the last monitors built for the United States Navy).

Source: Find A Grave, created by Shirley Stanton; Record added: Aug 31, 2003; Find A Grave Memorial# 7809640; Find a Grave – Christ Church at http://www.findagrave.com/cgi-bin/fg.cgi?page=gr&GRid=7809640

Major Stephen V.C. Van Renssalaer

Stephen V.C. Renssalaer (May 24, 1838 to May 20, 1885) is buried at Christ Church Cemetery, Belleville, N.J.

Renssalaer was a Union Army Officer in the Civil War. He was commissioned Captain and commander of Company A, 13th New Jersey Volunteer Infantry on August 22, 1861, and fought with his unit at the battles of Antietam, Fredericksburg, Chancellorsville and Gettysburg. On December 28, 1863 he was transferred to the 3rd New Jersey Volunteer cavalry, and was promoted to Major. Served with the cavalry until his resignation from the service on October 18, 1864.

Sources; Find a Grave – Christ Church Created by: Russ Dodge; Record added: May 9, 2002; Find A Grave Memorial# 640521; at http://www.findagrave.com/cgi-bin/fg.cgi?page=gr&GSsr=201&GScid=1259911&GRid=6405218&

Capt. Aaron Young

Captain Aaron Young died of typhoid fever at Belleville, on June 4, 1862. He served with Company F, Second Regiment, New Jersey Volunteer Infantry. Young joined the service on May 28, 1861. He is buried at Mount Pleasant Cemetery in Newark, N.J.

Sources: N.J. Civil War Record: Page 126, NEW JERSEY VOLUNTEERS. http://slic.njstatelib.org/...cations/civilwar/NJCWn126.html; Find a Grave Memorial Created by: Gregory Speciale; Record added: December 16, 2005; Find Grave Memorial # 12711282;

Diary of James C. Taylor

of Belleville, N.J.

In the War to Save the Union of the United States of America

Medal Grand Army of the Republic 1861 - Veteran - 1866

September 17th, 1864 - Enlisted in Captain John Hunkele's Co: F 39th Regiment, New Jersey Volunteers.

With me at the same time were enlisted John J. Rodgers, James M. Crisp, Linus Ackerman, Edmund Holmes, Charles Stanford, James McCluskey, Daniel McGinnis.

Sept. 19, 1864 All went to "Camp Frelinghuysen" on Roseville Ave., donned the Blue Uniform of the Union Army and all went home on a Pass.

Sept. 25 - Mustered into the United States Service.

Oct. 1st - In the evening we presented our Captain with a sword, sash, and belt; also our two Lieutenants.

Oct. 2nd - Got a pass and went home to see Mother and other friends. We were invited to the M. E. Church in the evening and each presented with a copy of the New Testament by the Pastor, Rev. D. R. Lowrie.

Oct. 3rd - Back in Camp by 9 A. M. and received a visit from several ladies, Mrs. Worthington, Mrs. Nuttall and others. At 5 P. M. a Dress Parade was held.

Oct. 4th - Marching Orders! Leave Camp at 9 A. M. Five Companies only, under the command of Lt. Col. James H.

Close marched down Broad St., and here I must digress. Leaving a widowed mother at home, and the main support being my brother, John, just recovering from Typhoid Fever, while sitting on the curb at Broad and Chestnut St., I thought of Mother, and was relieved that she did not appear to say good-bye, but it was better so. My mother was one of the best in the world in my estimation, and it would have saddened us both. Then some one touched me on the shoulder, I turned to look, and there was an elderly lady, - a cousin of my father's; she had trudged all down Broad St. to hand me a bag of cream puffs. I don't forget such acts as this, small as it may appear to others.

We finally resumed our March t0 the train at Chestnut St. Station, at 11 A. M. Locomotive got off the track at Elizabeth, got away at 4 P. M., arrived at Philadelphia at 10 P. M. where we were well fed by some of the best ladies at the aid Cooper Shop and off again at 1 A. M.

Oct. 5 - Arrived at Baltimore at 10 A. M. Stacked arms in street until 5 P. M., then marched into Fort Federal Hill and camped as well as we could, among the great guns which Gen. Butler had trained on the city long before. From here I mailed letters to my mother and my best girl.

Oct. 6 - 4 P. M. marched down to the docks and took the Transport, "Nellie Pentz" to City Point, Virginia.

Oct. 7 - Suspicions were aroused by the slow progress we were making down Chesapeake Bay and the engineer and the captain were put under arrest by an officer from the U. S. Gunboat "Dawn," who fired a shot, which caused our vessel to stop, and who declared us in distress. We were then taken in town by the "Steamer Lizzie" Baker at 2 P.M.

Oct. 8 - Anchored off Fortress Monroe last night. This morning put three (3) Companies on the Steamer George Weems, and off for City Point at last. At 11 A. M. passed the ruins of several houses at Harrison's Landing at 1 P. M. and at last arrived at City Point at 5 P. M., too late to land and go into Camp, so we were anchored out in the stream again.

Oct. 9 - Laid in the stream all last night. Landed at 9 A. M. New tents were issued to us and we went into camp on high ground in the afternoon.

Oct. 10 - Sent out to work on the breastworks with pick and shovel. I got sick ad was sent back to our camp. Ed. Holmes, and James Crisp are tenting with me; we call our tent the Hotel De Belleville.

Oct. 11 - Working on the trenches 8 hours a day and a gill of whiskey when we get through the day, for each man. Wrote to my best girl.

Oct. 12 - Still at work on the fortifications. About 11 A. M. the Engineer General rode by giving instructions; he looked more like a raw recruit, it was laughable to see him.

Oct. 13 - At the same work as before. Warm today, went to a farm house and got some butter milk, 2 canteens full.

Oct. 14 - Same work today but we take it easy. Some are complaining that they did not enlist to dig, and wish for a change. Most of us think the change will come soon enough.

Oct. 15th - This morning the program was changed, giving us a knapsack drill, worse a hundred times than the digging. We today also laid out our Co. Streets in the camp.

Oct. 16 - Today we had a Dress Parade and being Sunday, we had no work. Could hear heavy cannonading at Petersburg and Richmond. I begin to feel a sore throat, a case of "Quinsy."

Oct. 17 - Today it is worse and the Doctor excused me from all duty.

In the evening we could see the shells explode in the air up at the front.

Oct. 18 - Today our Colonel arrived and had his quarters put up, at 5 P. M. a Flag Raising and speeches by Col. & Lt. Col. My throat gets worse.

Oct. 19 - I am still off duty and can hardly eat or drink, am utterly miserable - my first attack of quinsy. Who wouldn't be a soldier?

Wrote a letter to Rev. Mr. Lowrie at Belleville.

Oct. 20 - Put on light camp duty today, about 1/2 hour work. Wrote to Rev. Mr. Smith, Bloomfield.

Oct. 21 - Again working in the trenches. In evening a large fire built in front of Col's tent and a prayer meeting held, very interesting indeed.

Oct. 22 - Went out to work as usual, but felt bad, throat worse and awful headache - our orderly sergeant told me to go into my tent, which I did.

Oct. 23 - This morning at 8 o'clock we broke camp and marched about five miles and took the box cars on Gen. Grant's Military railroad, got off at "Yellow Tavern," marched a few miles to Poplar Grove Church and encamped.

Oct. 24 - Spent the day putting up our tents, etc. so we now belong to the 1st Brigade and 2nd Division of the 9th Army Corps, Army of the Potomac, Major General John G. Parke, commanding.

Oct. 25 - Dress Parade 8:30 A. M., Company Drill, 10:30 to 11:30, then dinner. 2 P. M., Battalion Drill, then all at once marching orders, to where to we knew not.

Oct. 26 - Still in camp, expect to move soon.

Oct. 27 - At 2 A. M. as quiet as possible, we packed up everything and moved out toward the enemy. At daybreak General Meade and staff passed us, and the adjutant of our regiment joined us. Brisk firing down in the woods ahead of us, our regiment held in reserve. Here, I saw the wounded for the first time, some limping ... and blood" but able to walk, these were all the colored troops. Our regiment stood there, it seemed, for hours. I confess I felt rather shaky as I saw a fine looking officer brought near us, his left hip was horribly mangled and bloody. As the stretcher bearers were about to carry him further to the rear, he put his left hand down to feel the wound, then waved the right to us with a smile and a good-bye gentlemen.

Oct. 28 - Yesterday, I was with the regiment in another position in the evening turning one of the enemies abandoned breastworks and doing it in a heavy rain. That completed, I lay down for a little rest and sleep and slept from 2 to 4, then was called by the Corporal to go on duty as a Vidette and was placed down in the woods to watch and give alarm if I saw any thing, as the enemy was looked for in that direction. This whole movement was called a reconnaissance in force 3 or 4 Army Corps being engaged in it

Oct. 29 - We are back in our old camp and I am on the camp guard.

Nov. 10 - Brigade Drill lasting 3 hours - very tiresome.

Nov. 11 - News of Lincoln's re-election as President.

Nov. 13 - Letter from Brother John with some money and 24 post stamps.

Nov. 15 - Letter from Brother Henry enclosing money.

Nov. 17 - Brigade Drill.

Nov. 24 - Thanksgiving Day-Very little change in our dinner.

Nov. 27 - Went out to our picket line, curious to see how it looked and was told that Gen. Roger R. Pryon, Confederate, came into our line and gave himself up.

Nov. 28 - Battalion Drill by the Colonel.

Nov. 29 - Orders this A. M. for a General Review instead of which we packed up and marched down to front of Petersburg, laid in woods all night.

Nov. 30 - Laid out our Camp and pitched tents in the rear of "Fort Hell" and was known as "Camp Blackwater."

Dec. 3 - For the first time I am in the picket trenches: go on at 5 P. M. for 24 hours duty.

Dec. 4 - This is a bright and sunny morning, can hear the church bells in Petersburg; at 5 p. m. we are relieved by a new detail and return to our camp. A stray shot hits a man in camp.

Dec. 8 - A letter and photograph from my best girl.

Dec. 9 - On picket again and a cold hail and sleet storm, which froze to everything it touched. What a long, long night it was. I shall not forget it as long as life and mind last. My boots made to order before leaving home, costing $12.00, had to be cut off my feet. The Regiment during this time had gone on a mud march and suffered intensely.

Dec. 10 - The Regiment got back and were ordered out again and had to go and view the hanging of two young fellows of a N. Y. Regiment (Deserters).

Dec. 11 - Had a rest all day, it being Sunday, then had 24 more hours in the trenches - very cold and windy.

Dec. 15 - On Picket again.

Dec. 16 - The enemy throwing shells quite lively.

Dec. 18 - This morning our Forts are firing a salute for some recent victory.

Dec. 19 - On picket again, were shelled very lively, very difficult to get to our rifle pits.

Dec. 22 - Turned out in a hurry at 5 A. M. Nothing came of it.

Dec. 23 - Charley Stanford received a box of good things from his Belleville home.

Dec. 24 - Dan McGinnis went on Picket and had the end of one of his thumbs shot away. John Rodgers went on Picket with only 2 hardtack.

Dec. 25 - Christmas: Mailed Letters to Brother George, Henry Coeyman and John McCluskey. There is a scarcity of rations, even of hard tack.

Dec. 26 - A dispatch from Gen. Sherman read to the Regiment.

Dec. 27 - Battalion Drill today.

Dec. 28 - I am on Picket today with Rodgers and Holmes. Heavy shelling in afternoon, two shells came very near striking us as we went out by "Fort Hell."

Dec. 30 - I go on the Alarm Guard in afternoon.

Dec. 31 - Cold and stormy on Alarm Guard, which is a line of defense between our camp and the outer picket line. Came into camp at 4 P. M. mustered for pay and got some hot milk punch from our good Capt. John Hunkele.

1865

Jan. 3 - On Picket in same Rifle Pit with Private Klemme; who just at dusk was badly wounded in the shoulder, we believed by a sharp shooter. Holmes and Elder in same rifle pit.

Jan. 6 - Regiment ordered out to witness the execution of a deserter.

Jan. 9 - Wrote a letter to Polk Crisp's father to inform him that his son was on the sick list.

Jan. 13 - Went to Division Hospital to see Polk Crisp at the Division Hospital and found that he had been removed to the 9th Army Corps hospital at City Point. I received a letter for him from his father.

Jan. 17 - News of the capture of Fort Fisher and a salute fired at the enemy with shotted guns in honor of it.

Jan. 18 - At 5 P. M. go on picket in the trenches.

Jan. 22 - Received a welcome box of good things from mother with cigars and smoking tobacco from Mr. Gasherie DeWitt, of Belleville. Box had been broken in transit and the rain spoiled nearly all of it.

Jan. 29 - Today 1 am on the Alarm Guard. Mailed a letter of thanks to Mr. DeWitt, Belleville.

Jan. 31 - Regiment on monthly inspection. Mailed a letter to Bro. John, containing one to Cousin Mary, Bolton, England.

Feb. 1 - On Picket with Privates Deurr and McCluskey. In the afternoon there was great shouting and the pickets of both armies perched on top of their rifle pits. It turned out that a Flag of Truce was out, and (3) three Commissioners from the Confederate side were passing through our lines to confer with Lincoln and others to see what terms could be made to close the war - I shall never forget it.

Feb. 2 - I received a letter from Miss Annie Benson to James M. Crisp - 9th Corps. Hospital.

Feb. 3 - Sent the above and 3 other letters to him and one to his father at Belleville, N. J.

Feb. 5 - Capt. Hunkele returned from his furlough at his home in Newark, N. J. We received light marching orders and 4 days rations. Went to Church in evening and heard a Massachusetts chaplain.

Feb. 11 - We broke camp at Blackwater at 3 A. M. and occupied "Fort Davis" which was close by Had our quarters finished at 11 A. M.

Feb. 13 - Letter from G. DeWitt and Brother Henry.

Feb. 16 - A letter from Mr. Crisp to his son. Stanford and I procured passes on the Grand railroad to City Point and saw him there in our 9th Corps Hospital. While waiting for train, met our Lieut. Lange and he loaned be $2.00 without asking it, which was very welcome. I found that Crisp was well on the road to recovery but he said he did so much want the taste of an apple. I went out and after quite a search found a sutler with a few small ones and bought a half dozen. Now this was contrary to the surgeon's orders, but I sneaked them in to him. Many times since he told me that I saved his life.

Feb. 17 - A very heavy rain kept us all last night at the hospital and arrived back in camp at 12 noon and was called for the picket line at 4 P. M.

Feb. 20 - Cheer for the capture of Charleston, S. C., by Gen. Sherman's Army.

Feb. 22 - Washington's Birthday. Heavy shelling on the Appomatox (sic) River. Fort Mahone was opposite to us and for the first time they open fire on our relief of 100 on their way out to the trenches. No one was killed, but they had to scatter and finally got out all right.

Feb. 23 - At 11 P. M. saw quite a fire in Petersburg.

Feb. 24 - On Alarm Guard. A rainy night, 8 deserters came into our lines. Brisk shelling from both sides and our Regiment under arms most of the night.

Feb. 25 - Five months in the service today. It was reported that about 500 deserters came into our lines, 16 on our front. Signed pay roll and received $35.45.

Feb. 26 - Went down to Hancock Station and had a good square Dinner for $1.00. Saw about 70 deserters from the enemy.

March 4 - President takes the chair for 4 years more.

March 8 - Picked up a pocket book containing $9.25, advertised it as much as possible, so not finding an owner, used it.

March 15 - All sutlers are ordered to the rear which indicates a movement of some kind and go on Alarm Guard with Rodgers.

March 16 - All sutlers are moving back. Went to church in evening.

March 17 - Am on the picket lines again with Lance and Reiss. Singular occurrence during the evening - a half-grown toad hopped into our rifle pits and into our little fire which we always kept burning.

March 19 - A letter came to me to Crisp from his father and I mailed one to Dr. Arthur Ward, of Belleville. A new recruit came into my tent, from Newark, Louis Ayres, by name.

March 20 - Terrible shelling this P. M., our regiment just about formed for a Dress Parade, when the enemy spotted us and broke up the show. Our Major and Alonzo (Pop) Van Riper from Belleville, and our Left Guide of the regiment, had a close call from a shell which fell in the sand close to them, but failed to explode.

March 21 - A spy of the enemy caught in our lines last night. I am on camp guard today. Extra Pickets sent out tonight and John Duerr shot at 11 P. M. One Deserter in our guard house all night.

March 23 - Changed my residence to the next door with Obermann, Fruend and Veltpush. Heavy wind and trees blown down inside of our Fort Davis.

March 24 - A visit from Conrad Bein of the 40th N. J. Regiment Volunteers. Two deserters came into our lines and said we would be attacked before morning.

March 25 - At 4:30 A. M. the attack was made with 3 Brigades of the enemy, they got inside our lines, but were finally driven out with great loss and a great failure for General J. B. Gordon.

March 26 - Whole regiment turned out at 3 A. M. We then stacked arms and turned in again, but were told not to remove our equipment until the morning roll call.

March 27 - Sheridan's Cavalry came and encamped near us.

March 28 - Called out at 3:15 A. M. A visit from Jack McCluskey of the 3rd N. J. Cavalry, went on a Battalion Drill and were shelled by the enemy. On Alarm Guard in the afternoon, was placed to the left of Fort Davis and close by it. At 8 P. M. the long roll was beat and the regiment was under arms again; the climax seems to be near.

March 29 - The heavy picket firing last night which called the regiment out was caused by some deserters being fired on by their own side.

March 30 - Long roll beat last night at 10:30. Very rapid mortar shelling, under arms at 4 this A. M., go on picket in the trenches at 5 P. M.

March 31 - Our regiment posted in rear of Fort Rice until noon expecting an attack.

April 1 - At 11 last night 2 pieces of heavy artillery were brought into Fort Davis. This looks ominous. At 11:30 the regiment fell in and went out alongside the road where they waited there for hot coffee, and then we removed down to the front. We moved as far front as we could and then were ordered to lie flat on the ground. The enemy are firing lively with mortar shells and rifle shots. While lying flat, John Rogers received a fatal wound.

April 2 - At day-light the order to charge the enemy is given and we go and head for Fort Mahone, which we take and get inside but find they have a strong inner line and can get no further. Our Colonel orders us to retreat so we go back and use the front of the fort for a breastwork and hold the fort all day - at dusk - they retreated and never came back. The regiment retired at dusk to go back into our lines and into our home (Fort Davis) for the Night. Many of our regiment were killed and wounded. I had but one hour of sleep since coming off picket the previous day, so I slept like a stone on this night. I write home a few lines, all this was on Sunday - April 2nd.

April 3 - I am 22 today - yesterday I never expected to see it - go outside the Fort and see the pile of dead that had been brought in during the night, some of whom I recognized. One of the Belleville boys had been sent to the hospital but 5 days, then I saw Sergt. John Kehoe on a stretcher with one leg off. Michael McGuire, a Belleville man had gone out after dark and found him helpless, got him on his back and brought him in. It was a long distance to carry him. Now you can see what one comrade in the stress of war can do for another. Noble McGuire.

We are ordered to pack up after breakfast and leave Fort Davis, our late home, forever, and follow the retreating Confederates and just outside of Petersburg we are turned off the road, stacked our guns and rested for some time.

Our President Lincoln passed by on horseback with a small body guard. We all rushed to the roadside and greeted him. He has just crossed the very ground we had fought over the previous day. We had all gathered from rows of peach and pear trees near by, the pink and the white blossoms, which we made into small bouquets and put them in the muzzle of our guns, then we started off again and an the Brigade Music was massed in front. It was like a great moving bed of flowers.

As we approached the city we were greeted by 3 or 4 fine looking slaves I presume, but nearly white all of them. They waved their arms and called out, "Welcome Princes of Peace, we've been looking for yer dis long time but now wese looking right at yer." Then we passed on, all the drums playing "The Lass O' Gowrie," this I cannot ever forget - we soon passed through the city, it was at noon, and camped in a nice grove 10 miles away.

April 4 - 8 A. M. we go on the march again. During the day we met a rebel Brigade Gen. and Staff who are prisoners; go into camp at dark near a railroad, and here I discarded my overcoat.

April 5 - We resumed our march out following the Southside railroad. Now we meet a rebel Col. and 300 prisoners guarded by a company of our Cavalry. Sheridan is at our front and gives the enemy no rest.

April 6 - We are having a long march today and can hear the artillery firing which seems about 10 miles away. Pass Nottoway Court House and stop for the night about 11 P. M. This was the most lengthy and fatiguing march of my career, fully two thirds of the regiment fell out and took a rest on our own account, and most of these did not join the front until about 9 next morning. We finally get to Burksville Railroad Junction. Saw a lot of wounded "rebs" here. Saw, too, here a Union and Reb surgeon amputating limbs and they were very busy.

April 7 - We stop here all day. Holmes and I are drawn for picket duty.

April 8 - We draw rations. John Rodgers died today of his wounds.

April 9 - On the march again, and camp about 9 P. M.

April 10 - Off again at 7 A. M. and at noon we enter Farmville and cross a bridge into a paved street, the main street. As we got on to this pavement, a lone cavalry man passed and announced, "take your time boys! the War is over, Lee surrendered yesterday at 2 P. M. Many would not believe it. I was one that did. We turned off after a while and went into camp in a nice grove.

There was great joy at this news, and some of the boys went for a Fire Engine, got it out and paraded through the town cheering. Bells were rung wherever found. It was a hilarious time all the evening.

April 11 - Lee's men had to see the U. S. Provost Marshall, who occupied a place on the main street, there to sign a paper not to again take up arms. Then they had rations issued to all of them, which were very much needed.

April 12 - Saw the 6th, 2nd and part of the 25th Corps of our Army on their way back towards home. They made a grand sight for us.

April 13 - Men from Lee's army coming in here from all directions and I talked with several.

April 15 - Our Co. F were sent off on a special detail.

April 16 - Co. F got back at noon today. News that Gen. Johnston had surrendered to Sherman. Went to the M. E. Church at 2 P. M.

Heard that Pres. Lincoln had been shot.

April 18 - Part of the 24th Army Corps passed through on their way toward home. Dress Parade at 4:30 P. M., an Official Order was read of the death of President Lincoln by assassination.

April 19 - This is Wednesday, and is to be observed by all the U. S. Army, no work being done on account of funeral of Abraham Lincoln, the President.

April 20 - Eggs for breakfast. Struck out tents at 9 A. M. and marched back to Rice's Station, rested for dinner. Very hot and tiresome. Camp near Burkeville Junction for the night.

April 21 - Off again and reach Nottoway Court House at noon, I fell out and made coffee for dinner. My feet very sore, heard we were on the way to Washington, D.C., to be mustered out.

April 22 - Camped out last night 14 miles from Petersburg at the railroad water tank. There we slept on the ground.

April 23 - Sunday - Our 1st Brigade came along at 9 A. M. and we fell into our proper places and marched into Petersburg. A few of us went out to look over our battleground of April 2nd. This was where I expected to meet my death, but I really think an overruling power was watching over me at that time and also many times since.

April 24 - Off at 7 A. M. crossed the old lines of trenches near our Fort Steadman and camped at noon near City Point.

April 25 - Inspection of Arms and Knapsacks.

April 26 - Broke camp, went to the Point and took the steamer "Nereus."

April 27 - Sailed at Sunrise for Washington, D. C., passed Fortress Munroe at noon. Anchored in the mouth of the Potomac at night.

April 28 - At 4:30 A. M. off again; at Alexandria 3 P. M., go ashore and march to the High Ground at the back of the town and into camp.

April 29 - Received letters from home and one from Cousin Mary in Bolton, England.

April 30 - Inspection for muster at 11 A. M.

May 2 - James Crisp and I after our coffee started on foot for Mount Vernon, and saw "Washington's Tomb."

May 3 - Drilling all kinds now every day.

May 12 - Nothing of note until today - when in the evening all the camps lit up with candles.

May 13 - No drill today so cleaned and brightened up my rifle.

May 14 - News was received of the capture of Jefferson Davis and his staff at 9:30 A. M. and a brigade review at 3 P. M.

May 16 - Brigade Dress Parade. A quarrel broke out in Co. G. The fact is we are all getting tired of nothing but drill and want to be mustered out and start for home.

May 18 - We received news that a Grand Review of all the Army of the Potomac is ordered to be held in Washington on May 23rd, and the Western Army under Gen. Sherman on May 24th. Most all the regiment were sent down to guard paroled prisoners.

May 22 - Monday, Rose early to get ready for the march to the capital. Mailed a letter to my mother, and one other younger lady. Then we started on one more march to Washington, and arrived there at 12 noon. Stacked arms east of the Capitol and that was our camp for the night.

May 23 - This was the most wonderful parade that ever went down Pennsylvania Avenue, about 75,000 men and why? Because it was what was left of the Union Army. It drew to the reviewing stand in front of the White House many notable men from various parts of the world - President Lincoln was not there which caused a void in the hearts of the private soldiers now passing. It was now President Andrew Johnson. Our Regiment marched 16 files front, 32 to each Co. It received its first "Baptism of Fire" on the 2nd of April, 1865.

May 25 - 8 months in the service today.

May 28 - Helped Lawrence Burns to Hospital.

May 30 - Am on guard at Brigade Headquarters today.

May 31 - Visit from Joe Brooks and Jack McCluskey. Went down to the Potomac River for a swim. Marcus L. Ward, of Newark, known as the soldiers' friend, also visited our regiment and made a speech,

June 1 - Roberts, McCluskey and I walked down to Mt. Vernon and visited Washington's Tomb.

June 2 - Went fishing with Sam Hampson, got no fish; he tried to jab a water snake with his knife but was bitten on the thumb.

June 3 - A review of our 2nd Division today.

June 4 - Inspection at 7 A. M. Very hot.

June 5 - Brigade Review at 6 P. M. By our old Commander John G. Curtin, in tears as he rode along at his farewell.

June 6 - Our Company got its muster out roll. Looks like home. In the evening the 36th Mass. Regiment serenaded the 45th Pennsylvania and other Regiments of our Brigade as they were to leave for home.

June 7 - Our muster out rolls are being made today.

June 9 - 35th Mass. Regiment left for home this A. M. Our Regiment fell in and cheered them.

June 10 - The 7th Rhode Island and 36th Mass. left for home today. Our Col. Wildrick is acting Brigadier General.

June 11 - Got a pass to go to Alexandria - Saw Larry Burns in hospital there. Met his father also.

June 12 - A visit of 3 members of the 3rd N. J. Cavalry, John McCluskey, John McDonald and Lt. Ackerman.

June 13 - A good square meal of beef steak and onions was enjoyed by Polk Crisp and me tonight.

June 14 - Two members of our Company caught a live eagle and brought it into camp.

June 17 - The recruits which came to us were transferred to the 33rd N.J. Regiment. At about 1 P. M. the 39th was mustered out and we expect to leave for home tomorrow.

June 18 - Last night we had a grand illumination and paid our respects to the other regiments of the brigade. At midnight we turned in and so on to Washington, D.C. Took train to Baltimore arrived by the 4th and 7th R.I. Regiments, marched down to Alexandria our tents and at 6 A. M. left our last camp in Virginia, escorted there 2 P. M.

June 19 - Arrived in Philadelphia at 11:30 A. M. Had a good meal at the "Old Cooper Shop," attended by the ladies of the city. In the early evening we marched through the streets, where we were greatly cheered by the ladies especially, windows were all occupied and our eagle was carried on a perch and caused quite a sensation. We then took the train and arrived at Trenton. Marched out of station to a vacant spot near by. Stacked our guns and awaited a breakfast which the ladies of the vicinity served to us. We later on marched down State street, Trenton. Gov. Parker had invited m all to a luncheon at noon and made a speech of welcome.

June 20 - I arrived home in Belleville at 7:30 P. M. had a thorough bath and donned my citizen suit and made a call on one outside my own family.

In conclusion will say that I had a good (yes a very good) Captain in John Hunkele of Newark, N. J., and notwithstanding all the dangers and hardships that I successfully passed through, I did not get as much as a scratch. "Close Call," yes several that I was aware of at the time, and I am the only one left of the eight that enlisted from Belleville, N. J.

JAMES C. TAYLOR.
Aug. 24, 1925.

Presented to Belleville Historical Society, 1971,
by Anna Underwood.
De Witt Press Print
115 Roseville Avenue
Newark, N.J.

39th Regiment - Infantry - Volunteers

The 39th Regiment was organized under the provisions of an Act of Congress, approved July 22, 1861, and an Act of Congress, approved July 4, 1864, as set forth in General Orders No. 224, dated War Department, Adjutant General's Office, Washington, D. C., July 6, 1864, and under authority received from the War Department for the raising of two regiments of Infantry, and promulgated in General Orders No. 4, dated Office of Adjutant General, Trenton, N. J., August 24, 1864.

The Regiment was organized under the provisions of General Orders No. 110, War Department, Adjutant General's Office, Washington, D. C., April 29, 1863. Instructions were issued and recruiting for the Regiment immediately commenced.

The Headquarters of the Regiment was established at Camp Frelinghuysen, Newark, N. J., and active measures were put forth to complete the organization at an early day.

The required number of men to complete the Regiment was soon raised and mustered into the service of the United States, by companies, for one year.

Company A was mustered in October 11; Company B, September 30; Company C, October 8; Company D, October 3; Company E, September 23; Company F, September 25; Company G, September 23; Company H, September 26; Company I, October 1; Company K, September 23, 1864, at Camp Frelinghuysen, Newark, N. J., by William O. Douglass, Second Lieutenant, Fourteenth Infantry, United States Army.

Soon after the commencement of this regiment, authority was issued for the raising of another regiment of Infantry, to be known as the 41st, recruiting being dull it failed of success - the men that had been enlisted for it were transferred to and joined this regiment.

The Regiment was fully completed and organized by the 11th day of October, 1864, having a full complement of men.

Officers, 39; Non-Commissioned Officers and Privates, 973.

Total, 1012.

It left the State by detachments. Companies E, F, G, H, and K, left October 4, 1864, under the command of Lieutenant-Colonel James H.

Close; Company D, left October 9th, under the command of Captain Fowler Merrill; Companies B and I, left October 10th, under the command of Major William T. Cornish, and Companies A, C, and Field and Staff, left October 14, 1864, under the command of Colonel Abram C. Wildrick, and proceeded under orders direct to the front.

Arriving at City Point, Va., it was temporarily assigned to duty with General Benham's Brigade of Engineers, within the fortifications around Petersburg.

It remained in this connection but a short time; when it was assigned to the Ninth Army Corps. During the months of March and April, 1865, the strength of the Regiment was increased by the joining from Draft Rendezvous, Trenton, N. J., of a large number of recruits.

The Regiment continued its organization and remained in active service until the close of the war, and those not entitled to discharge under the provisions of General Orders No. 77, War Department, Adjutant General's Office, Washington, D. C., April 28, 1865, were transferred to the Thirty-third Regiment, in compliance with Special Orders No. 45, dated Headquarters, Ninth Army Corps, June 15, 1865, and were discharged with that regiment.

The remainder were mustered out of service near Alexandria, Va., June 17, 1865, under provisions of special orders from War Department, Adjutant General's Office, Washington, D. C., dated May 18, 1865, by Edward Rose, First Lieutenant Fifty-sixth Infantry, Massachusetts Volunteers, Assistant Commissary of Musters, Second Division, Ninth Army Corps.

The Regiment was first attached to General Benham's Brigade of Engineers, Army of the James - then to the First Brigade, Second Division, Ninth Army Corps.

The Regiment took part in the following engagements: Before Petersburg, Va., (Capture of Fort Mahone), April 2, 1865.

Source: NJ State Library, NJ Civil War Record, Page 1129

Nutley (Franklin) Men Killed In Action

James H. Cunningham

Private James H. Cunningham was killed in action on May 3, 1863, in the Second Battle of Fredericksburg, also known as the Second Battle of Marye's Heights, in Fredericksburg, Va., as part of the Battle of Chancellorsville, or the Chancellorsville Campaign (April-May 1863).

On May 1, Gen. Robert E. Lee left Maj. Gen. Jubal A. Early's division to hold Fredericksburg, while marching with the rest of the army to meet Hooker's main offensive thrust at Chancellorsville. On May 3, the Union VI Corps under Sedgwick, reinforced by John Gibbon's II Corps division, having crossed the Rappahannock River, assaulted and carried the Confederate entrenchments on Marye's Heights. The outnumbered Confederates withdrew and regrouped west and southeast of town.

Cunningham served with the New Jersey Volunteers, Company C, 26th Regiment. He is buried at National Cemetery, Fredericksburg, Va., Div. B, Sec. B, Grave 209.

Sources: N.J. Civil War Record: Page 845; N.J. Civil War Record: Page 1751 BURIAL RECORD OF NEW JERSEY SOLDIERS. National Park Service http://www.cr.nps.gov/hps/abpp/battles/va034.htm; Wikipedia http://en.wikipedia.org/wiki/Second_Battle_of_Fredericksburg

Sgt. John Donaldson

Sergeant John Donaldson died May 17, 1862, of wounds received in action at Williamsburg, Va.

The Battle of Williamsburg, also known as the Battle of Fort Magruder, took place on May 5, in York County, James City County, and Williamsburg, Va.

In the first pitched battle of the Peninsula Campaign, nearly 41,000 Federals and 32,000 Confederates were engaged. Following up the Confederate retreat from Yorktown, Hooker's division encountered the Confederate rearguard near Williamsburg. Hooker assaulted Fort

Magruder, an earthen fortification alongside the Williamsburg Road, but was repulsed. Confederate counterattacks, directed by Maj. Gen. James Longstreet, threatened to overwhelm the Union left flank, until Kearny's division arrived to stabilize the Federal position. Hancock's brigade then moved to threaten the Confederate left flank, occupying two abandoned redoubts. The Confederates counterattacked unsuccessfully. Hancock's localized success was not exploited. The Confederate army continued its withdrawal during the night.

He joined the service on August 28, 1861 and served with the New Jersey Volunteers, Company C, 7th Regiment.

Source: N.J. Civil War Record: Page 320; National Park Service http://www.cr.nps.gov/hps/abpp/battles/va010.htm; Wikipedia http://en.wikipedia.org/wiki/Battle_of_Williamsburg;

Byron Lawton

Private Byron Lawton was killed in action at Crampton's Pass, Md., on September 14, 1862, in the Battle of South Mountain, or the Battle of Burkittsville in Central Maryland during the Maryland Campaign.

Tactically the battle resulted in a Union victory because they broke the Confederate line and drove through the gap. Strategically, the Confederates were successful in stalling the Union advance

He joined the service on February 19, 1862 and served with the New Jersey Volunteers, Company I, 2nd Regiment.

Source: N.J. Civil War Record: Page 144; Wikipedia http://en.wikipedia.org/wiki/Battle_of_Crampton%27s_Gap; The Battle of Antietam on the Web http://antietam.aotw.org/exhibit.php?exhibit_id=421

In honor of the men of Franklin
who served in the war of 1861 - 1865

Harry Ackerman
Joseph Baldwin
James Blair
Enoch Booth
Hiram M. Booth
Frank Brown
Garrett Brown
Herman Brown
Henry Brown
Hiram Brown
Oliver Brown
Samuel M. Brown
Stephen Brown
James Calhoun
Bryan Carroll
William Clark
Thomas Coffee
William Conover
Thomas Conover
Thomas Conover Jr.
John Corb
Richard V. Cueman
James H. Cunningham, KIA
John Cunningham
Sefferine Dailey
Robert Day
Joshua W. Dodd
John Donaldson, KIA
William Flemming

Michael Gaffney

John Garrabrant

Robert Guile

Richard Guile

Ezekiell Guile

A.M. Hallidy

John Hanily

Thomas Hennen

Charles Jacobus

David Jenkins

Frederick Jenkins

James Jenkins

George Kingsland

John Kipp

Jacob Labaugh

Robert Law

Byron Lawton, KIA

Cornelius McClees

David McGirr

James McGirr

Horace Mesler

Frank Nevey

William Nevey

Charles A. Pierce

George Pollock

Henry G. Prout

William E. Queman

Abraham Riker

Jacob Riker

Calvin Rutan

James R. Rutan

William Sargent

J.F. Satterthwaite

J.S. Satterthwaite

William H. Speer

Abraham H. Stager

Garrett Stager

George H. Stager

William H. Stager

George Surgent

George W. Symonds

Thomas H. Travers

Robert P. Travis

Simon Tuers

Henry M. Vreeland

Stephen P. Vreeland

Robert Wallace

Samuel H. Ward

Robert Williams

Sources: Civil War Memorial, Franklin Avenue, Nutley, N.J.; Charles Hammond, NUTLEY Yesterday – Today, Nutley Historical Society, Nutley, N.J., 1961

IN HONOR OF
THE MEN OF FRANKLIN
WHO SERVED IN THE WAR OF
1861 — 1865

HENRY ACKERMAN	SEFFRINE DAILEY	HORRACE MESLER
JOSEPH BALDWIN	JOHN DONALDSON	DAVID McGIRR
ENOCH BOOTH	JOSHUA W. DODD	JAMES McGIRP
HIRAM M. BOOTH	WILLIAM FLEMMING	CHARLES A. PIERCE
HENRY BROWN	MICHAEL GAFFNEY	ABRAHAM RIKER
FRANK BROWN	JOHN GARRABRANT	J.F. SATTERTHWAITE
HIRAM BROWN	ROBERT GUILE	J.S. SATTERTHWAITE
OLIVER BROWN	RICHARD GUILE	WILLIAM H. SPEER
STEPHEN BROWN	EZEKIEL GUILE	ABRAHAM H. STAGER
BRYAN CARROLL	JOHN HANILY	GARRETT STAGER
JAMES CALHOUN	FRANK HEVEY	GEORGE H. STAGER
WILLIAM CONOVER	WILLIAM HEVEY	WILLIAM H. STAGER
THOMAS CONROY	THOMAS HENNEN	THOMAS H. TRAVERS
THOMAS CONROY JR.	CHARLES JACOBUS	SIMON TUERS
JOHN CORB	DAVID JENKINS	HENRY M. VREELAND
THOMAS COFFEE	FREDERICK JENKINS	STEPHEN P. VREELAND
JAMES H. CUNNINGHAM	GEORGE KINGSLAND	SAMUEL H. WARD
JOHN CUNNINGHAM	JOHN KIPP	ROBERT WALLACE
RICHARD V. CUEMAN	ROBERT LAW	
ROBERT DAY	BYRON LAWTON	

ERECTED BY
THE PUPILS OF
THE NUTLEY PUBLIC SCHOOLS
MCMVIIII

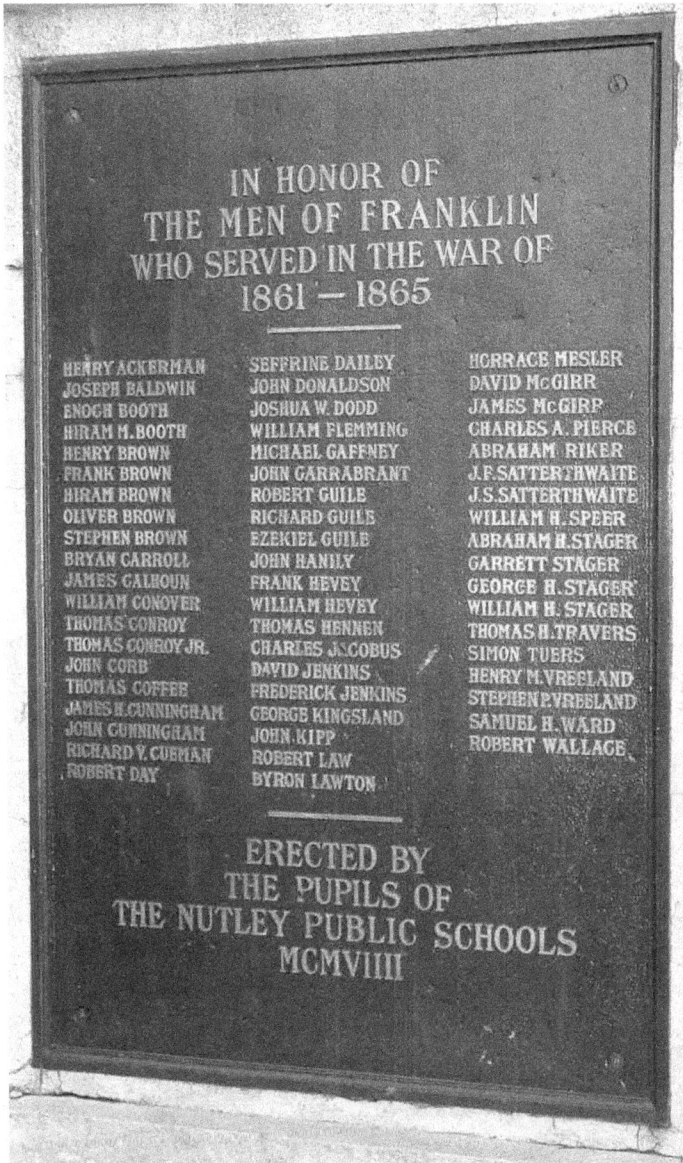

(May 25, 1958) - The new Civil War Memorial in front of the Junior High School auditorium will be formally dedicated during Memorial Day ceremonies on Friday morning. The bronze plaque was originally set in boulder at the corner of Franklin Avenue and New Street but made way for the Junior High School classroom addition. This plaque containing 55 names of Nutley men who served in the Civil War has been refurbished. It was presented to the Board of Education by school children in 1909. The memorial is built of Tennessee marble. (*The Nutley Sun*)

On Far-Flung Battlefields Nutley's Sons Died

FROM FRANK SPEER

The long War of Secession saw 58 men leave Nutley; all but three came back. To its glory, Nutley, then but a town of 1,500 population, escaped President Lincoln's 1862 draft by furnishing a number of volunteers greater than her draft quota.

For a half-century after the return of the volunteers from the Civil War, they marched every Memorial Day and established a tradition which carried on long after the last of the warriors of the War of Emancipation had died.

Even after World War I, there were still a few Civil War veterans to parade on Decoration Day, although they rode in carriages or in cars from the Methodist cemetery to the Reformed cemetery and, in keeping with a simple tradition, planted a bright new flag and geraniums on the grave of every soldier, not overlooking the burial place in the old Dutch cemetery in Brookdale of Major Isaac Kierstead, one of Nutley's few volunteers against the return of the British in 1812.

Stephen Vreeland, one of the town's few officers in the Civil War, was the traditional grand marshal. A stately man, he used to lead the Memorial Day parades on a white horse, a sword slung at his side by a red sash. With his death, the few survivors gave up marching and the veterans of the Spanish-American War and the First World War took up the tradition.

When Abraham Lincoln freed the slaves and the Southern States seceded, Nutley was ardently abolitionist. It took time, however, for the town to get the war spirit. None of Nutley's eventual 58 volunteers was a "three months' man," those soldiers of the First New Jersey Brigade who were the first to arrive for the defense of Washington and were held in reserve there during the Battle of Bull Run.

The First Brigade, called the "Jersey Blues," was composed chiefly of Newark militiamen, although there was an entire company, Company F, recruited in Belleville. It commander was Brigadier-General Theodore Runyon, who owed his sudden promotion in life to an act of Governor Charles Olden. Equipped by the state, it was the first fully equipped brigade to reach Washington for the capital's defense. Moving the brigade was quite a problem and it finally had to travel by canal boat on the Delaware and Chesapeake Canal from Trenton to Annapolis, making the trip in six days.

The First Brigade sat on a hill as reserves and watched the stampede of Bull Run, the first great battle and the first disgraceful rout of the Union troops. Later it was to see stiff fighting all the way from Antietam to Fredericksburg, Gettysburg, Cold Harbor, Petersburg, Manassas to Lee's surrender at Appomattox-the full campaign of Virginia.

It was only after General Robert E. Lee invaded Pennsylvania that Nutley became alarmed. Henry Stager, "Big Abe" Stager, Simon Tuers, Silas Chappell, Bob Day, John Dodd, Jim Blair, and Hiram Van Winkle rose in their anger at the invasion and walked all the way to Newark where they enlisted "en masse."

Another military company of 40 men was formed here under Cornelius McClees and went into training at the Old Military Hall. It was there that McClees gave them their first lessons in the manual of arms. They learned the simple squad movements on what is now a corner of the High School playground.

One morning, when McClees was satisfied that his trainees were ready, he marched 26 of them down to Newark and they joined up, forming the nucleus of Company C, 26th New Jersey Volunteer Regiment. They were still raw recruits, however, when they fought in three engagements before the Battle of Fredericksburg as part of the army of General Burnside who took a terrible beating in mid-December 1862, but they learned the art of war and the following spring took and held the heights of Fredericksburg.

The 26th regiment, which had companies from Newark, Caldwell, Bloomfield, and the Oranges, as well as Nutley, was mustered at Camp Frelinghuysen on September 3, 1862, at the very same time that the disgraceful draft riots were taking place in Newark and New York

It was a "nine-months' regiment" which saw action at Fredericksburg, Salem Heights and Franklin's Crossing before it was mustered out. After waiting out Burnside's indecision in the woods near Fredericksburg, the Nutley soldiers proved gallant in action in the affair at Franklin's Crossing just a short time before the term of enlistment expired.

When the Confederates had been shelled out of their positions across the Rappahannock, below Fredericksburg, two regiments-the 26th and the 5th Vermont-were ordered to take boats and cross the river to capture the rebel position. It was a boat race and the 26th won, capturing a big bag of prisoners.

Seven other Nutley men were members of the 39th New Jersey Volunteers and had their share of fighting, principally in Virginia, where they joined in the long siege of Petersburg (1864) and assisted in the capture of Fort Mahone (1865).

Four other Nutley volunteers fought with an elite regiment, the First New York Mounted Rifles.

Many Nutley and other Essex volunteers went to New York to enlist because there were too many volunteers to be absorbed speedily by the New Jersey regiments. Others went as units, piqued by delays or accusing New Jersey military authorities of playing politics. Captain Toler took his company of elite militia, known as the Montgomery Guards, to New York and enlisted in Sickle's famous Excelsior Brigade (71st N.Y. regiment), blaming "politics" when his company was refused a place in the First Brigade. Four other Essex militia companies joined the defection and fought gallantly with the Excelsiors.

George Symonds, who volunteered in the 12th N.Y. "Old Guard" and was taken, even though he was under age, became an orderly to General Warren. He served with him all through the battles from the Wilderness to Petersburg.

When the war ended, he returned to the Oxford Academy and then went to Cornell. He then came to Nutley and was for 17 years the first school principal. For seven years he was the town engineer.

Although they saw plenty of fighting, Nutley's sons came through the Civil War with comparatively light losses. Only three were killed in action: James Cunningham, John Donaldson, and Byron Lawton. The 26th regiment lost an officer and 35 men in its long service, while the 39th lost three officers and 36 men, most of them buried in war cemeteries throughout the South.

Source: Frank Speer, in Nutley Yesterday-Today, On Far-Flung Battlefield's Nutley's Sons Have Died, Pages 44 to 47

Call For Volunteers

The call for volunteers in 1862 found Franklin a part of Belleville. A small military company of about forty men had been drilling for some time under Cornelius McClees, in the old school house on Avondale Road.

Twenty-six of this little company immediately volunteered and with fourteen others from Belleville marched with McClees to Newark to Camp Frelinghuysen. The camp served as rendezvous and drill ground for volunteer regiments of the state. According to a commemorative plaque at the site, it lay within the tract bounded by the Morris Canal, Orange Street, Roseville and Bloomfield avenues.

Here they were mustered into the State Service on September 3, 1862, and were enrolled in Company C of the 26th New Jersey Volunteers for nine months.

The regiment was made up of men from adjoining towns, Orange, South Orange, Bloomfield and Caldwell, each furnishing one company, while Newark furnished the remaining six.

Three weeks later, after they were officered and equipped, they proceeded to Washington.

Samuel H. Pemberton, of Newark, was chosen captain of Company C and Cornelius McClees First Lieutenant.

The "26th of New Jersey" was in three engagements before Fredericksburg, the great defeat of the Union troops, under General Burnside, on December 13, 1862, and the two minor engagements of May 3 and June 5, 1863, under General Hooker.

In the great battle of Dec. 13th, as raw troops, they faced the terrific fire of the Confederate batteries, and for three nights lay down upon their arms.

They also took part in the memorable "mud march" back to Camp.

After the season in winter quarters near Belle Plain they again took the field, and eventually captured and held the Heights of Fredericksburg.

The regiment returned to Newark when their term of enlistment expired and was mustered out Sept. 19, 1863.

Seven Franklin men were enrolled in the 39th New Jersey Volunteers.

They enlisted at Newark from Camp Frelinghuysen and left for the South in detachments, in October 1864.

The 39th Regiment was in the long and terrible siege of Petersburg and assisted in the capture of Fort Mahone, April 2, 1865.

A part of the regiment was transferred to the 33rd New Jersey Volunteers, and discharged with that regiment.

The remainder were mustered out near Alexandria, Va., June 17, 1865.

Four Franklin men were enlisted in the 1st New York Mounted Rifles.

The companies forming this regiment were organized in New York State and mustered into service in 1861 and 1862.

The 1st New York Mounted Rifles took part in the operations against Petersburg and Richmond, and in a great number of minor engagements. In 1865, they were consolidated into the 3rd New York Calvary Regiment, forming the 4th Provisional Calvary.

Source: The History of Nutley, compiled by Elizabeth Stow Brown, The Woman's Public School Auxiliary; copyright 1907 by The Board of Education of Nutley, New Jersey.

Veterans of Nutley

The names of the men of Franklin who fought in the struggle for the Union are here given in a list that has been carefully revised. Before many years it is to be hoped that some imperishable memorial may honor these names and keep them constantly before the younger generations whose country they helped to preserve. To the names of those who enlisted from Franklin are added a number of residents who enlisted elsewhere, and a few veterans who have become residents here since the war.

Men of Nutley (Franklin) in the Civil War

26th Regiment, New Jersey Volunteers, Co. C

First Lt. – Cornelius McClees

First Sgt. – George H. Stager

Corporals – Joshua W. Dodd, James R. Rutan, also in 2nd NY, Harris Light Cavalry

Privates – Harry Ackerman, James Blair, Hiram M. Booth, Garrett Brown, Henry Brown, Stephen Brown, Robert Day, Frederick Jenkins, James McGirr, Horace Mesler, William E. Queman, Abraham Riker, Jacob Riker, Calvin Rutan, Abraham H. Stager, William H. Stager, George Surgent, George Kingsland, James H. Cunningham (killed at Fredericksburg), Simon Tuers, Robert Williams, Jacob Labaugh, Richard V. Cueman, Thomas Hennen.

39th Regiment, New Jersey Volunteers

Privates – John Corb (also in 25th NJV), David Jenkins, Enoch Booth, John Hanily, John Garrabrant, Michael Gaffney, Garrett L. Stager.

1st New York

Mounted Rifles
Samuel M. Brown, George Pollock, William H. Speer, Herman Brown

Frankin Men Who Enlisted in Other Regiments

Bryan Carroll, David McGirr, Hiram Brown, 10th Reg. NJV,

Stephen P. Vreeland, 2nd Reg. NYV Calvary, John Donaldson (died in service), James Jenkins, 3rd Reg. NJ Calvary, Charles A. Pierce, *Byron Lawton (Died in Action),* William Sargent, William Conover, J. Fisher Satterthwaite, 7th Reg. NYV and 22nd Reg. NJV, Charles Jacobus, William Fleming

Other Resident Veterans

Robert P. Travis, 9th 83rd and 94th NYV; A. M. Hallidy, 2nd Reg. District of Columbia

William Clark; George W. Symonds, 12th NYV; Henry G. Prout, 57th Mass. Infantry

For some years a Veterans' Association was maintained in this town. Many of the residents belonged to Garfield Post, Newark.

Source: The History of Nutley, compiled by Elizabeth Stow Brown, The Woman's Public School Auxiliary; copyright 1907 by The Board of Education of Nutley, New Jersey.

Acknowledgements

Angelo Buccino, Russell Roemmele

Dr. Andrea Buccino, Dawn Buccino. Harry and Nancy Vincenti.

Belleville Public Library: Joan Taub, director; Reference desk: Fred Lewis and Cindy LaRue

Nutley Public Library: JoAnne Tropiano, Director; Senior Reference Librarian Kiran Patel; and reference librarians Deborah D'Ambrosio and Jeanne Sylvester

The Belleville Historical Society

The Nutley Historical Society

Newark Public Library, Charles F. Cummings

Ed Stecewicz

Joseph T. Fornarotto

Norman Price

Glen Pierce

Michael Perrone

Dave Hinrichs

Lucille and Rodger Gustafson; Peter and Donna Gustafson

Salvatore and Sharon Buttaci

Books

Ambrose, Stephen E.

-*Americans At War*, Berkley Books, New York 1998

-*Band of Brothers*, Touchstone, New York, 1992

-*Comrades*, Simon & Schuster, New York, 1999

-*Citizen Soldiers*, Touchstone, New York, 1997

-*D-Day June 6, 1944: The Climactic Battle of World War II*, Touchstone, Simon & Schuster, New York 1994

-*To America, Personal Reflections of an Historian* Simon & Schuster, New York, 2002

-*Undaunted Courage, Meriwether Lewis, Thomas Jefferson, and the Opening of the American West* Simon & Schuster Paperbacks, New York, 1996

Baker, Russell, *Growing Up*

Bennett, Jeffrey - Newarkology, http://www.newarkhistory.com/branchbrooklake.html

Bilby, J. - http://newarktalk.com/talk/viewtopic.php?p=12435&sid=4cb043f39fa5 66d8084125738f2b455a

Buccino, Anthony and Andrea,

- *Nutley Sons Honor Roll – remembering the men who paid for our freedom* Cherry Blossom Press, 2004, 2009

- *Belleville Sons Honor Roll – remembering the men who paid for our freedom* Cherry Blossom Press, 2004, 2009

Burnett, Robert B., and the Belleville 150th-Anniversary Committee Belleville *Belleville: 150th-Anniversary Historical Highlights 1839-1989 Belleville, New Jersey. 1991*

Canfora, Nicole T. *Images of America – Belleville*, Arcadia, Charleston, S.C., 2002

Cox, Hank H. *Lincoln and the Sioux Uprising of 1862* Cumberland House Publishing, Nashville, Tenn. 2005

Davis, Burke *The Civil War Strange & Fascinating Facts* Wings Books, New York, 1960

Demmer, John *Images of America – Nutley*, Arcadia, Dover, N.H., 1997

Hammond, Charles, quoted in *NUTLEY Yesterday – Today* Nutley Historical Society, Nutley, N.J., 1961

Kagan, Norman *The War Film*, Pyramid Illustrated History of the Movies, Pyramid Communications, New York, 1974

Kindre, Tom *The Boys From New Jersey*, Trafford, 2004

LoCurcio III, Vincent, and **Fred Van Steen, Jean Van Steen, Marilyn Peters, Rich O'Connor** *One Hundred Years of Nutley Celebrating Our Town's First Century 1902-2002* Nutley Centennial Gala Committee, Nutley, N.J., 2002.

Pascrell Jr., Congressman William, 300TH ANNIVERSARY OF THE BELLEVILLE REFORMED CHURCH – Congressional Record, March 10, 1997.

Price, Norman, Second River historian, http://secondriver.blogspot.com/

Pyle, Ernie

-*Brave* Men Aeonian Press Mattituck, N.Y., republished 1978

-*Here is Your War* Ayer, North Stratford, N.H., Reprint edition 1998

-*Typewriter Soldier* Carter, Horace W., and Faircloth Rudy; Atlantic Publishing Co. Tabor City, N.C., 1982

Speer, Frank

On Far-Flung Battlefields Nutley's Sons Have Died, in *NUTLEY Yesterday – Today* Nutley Historical Society, Nutley, N.J., 1961

Nutley Was Born in Strife, Strategy and Secession, in *NUTLEY Yesterday – Today* Nutley Historical Society, Nutley, N.J., 1961

Spohn, Jule Jan. 15, 2008, transcript of Camp Frelinghuysen plaque http://newarktrivia.com/trivia/viewtopic.php?p=64059&sid=07767c2ed 1a623fc08c386bd8a88cd97

Stow Brow, Elizabeth, *The History of Nutley*, The Woman's Public School Auxiliary; copyright 1907 by The Board of Education of Nutley, New Jersey.

Taylor, James C., *Civil War Diary of James C. Taylor*, Belleville, 1925

Tobin, James *Ernie Pyle's War – America's Eyewitness to World War II* University of Kansas Press, Lawrence, Kan., 1997

Troy, Ann A., *NUTLEY Yesterday – Today* Nutley Historical Society, Nutley, N.J., 1961

Libraries

Belleville Public Library

Camden County Library, Jennifer Whelan

Newark Public Library New Jersey Information Center

Nutley Public Library

South Brunswick Public Library

Other Sources and References

American Battle Monuments Commission www.abmc.gov

American Civil War http://americancivilwar.com/statepic/va/va021.html

American Legion www.legion.org

Amvets www.amvets.org

Belleville-Nutley DAV Chapter 22, Joseph T. Fornarotto

Civil War Index http://www.civilwarindex.com/newjersey.html

Civil War 1861-1865 www.njstatelib.org

Congressional Record, 105th Congress (1997-1998), 300th Anniversary of the Belleville Reformed Church – Hon. Bill Pascrell, Jr. (Extension of Remarks - March 10, 1997)

National Park Service

- http://www.nps.gov/cwdw/planyourvisit/brochures.htm
- http://www.nps.gov/cwdw/historyculture/index.htm
- http://www.nps.gov/cwdw/historyculture/fort-davis.htm
- http://www.nps.gov/cwdw/historyculture/index.htm

Newark Daily Mercury, August 13, 1962

New Jersey Historical Society

New Jersey in the American Civil War,
http://en.wikipedia.org/wiki/New_Jersey_in_the_American_Civil_War

New Jersey State Library Cyberdesk

QandANJ.org

Reformed Dutch Church of Second River, Belleville, N.J.

Wikipedia

- http://en.wikipedia.org/wiki/Seven_Days_Battles#Gaines.27s_Mill
- http://en.wikipedia.org/wiki/Battle_of_Williamsburg
- http://en.wikipedia.org/wiki/Second_Battle_of_Fredericksburg
- http://en.wikipedia.org/wiki/Battle_of_Crampton%27s_Gap
- http://creativecommons.org/licenses/by-sa/3.0/

About the Editor

Anthony Buccino

Writer/editor/web designer Anthony Buccino has written five books based in and around Nutley and Belleville, New Jersey, where he has lived for six decades.

With his daughter, Andrea Buccino, he created the Nutley Sons and Belleville Sons honor roll web sites and books recounting the lives and service of more than 300 local men who died in service to their country.

Buccino has been published in New Jersey Monthly, the Wall Street Journal, the Passaic Herald News and other publications.

He attended Holy Family School in Nutley, School 10 in Belleville and both the junior and senior high schools in Belleville. He attended Montclair State College where he majored in English and minored in journalism.

Buccino published and continues to write essays and poetry based on his memories of growing up on the Nutley-Belleville border. He is an award-winning blogger and has been nominated for Pushcart Prize.

In 1990 he edited The Belleville Times. In the mid-90s, he was managing editor at Worrall Community Newspapers, Bloomfield, overseeing The Belleville Post and the Nutley Journal.

Buccino maintains OldBelleville.org and OldNutley.org, two history and information web sites.

http://www.anthonybuccino.com/

Please share your comments

A Buccino
PO Box 110252
Nutley NJ 07110

www.ingramcontent.com/pod-product-compliance
Lightning Source LLC
Chambersburg PA
CBHW071343290326
41933CB00040B/2143